797,885 Books

are available to read at

www.ForgottenBooks.com

Forgotten Books' App
Available for mobile, tablet & eReader

ISBN 978-1-334-28871-5
PIBN 10593945

This book is a reproduction of an important historical work. Forgotten Books uses state-of-the-art technology to digitally reconstruct the work, preserving the original format whilst repairing imperfections present in the aged copy. In rare cases, an imperfection in the original, such as a blemish or missing page, may be replicated in our edition. We do, however, repair the vast majority of imperfections successfully; any imperfections that remain are intentionally left to preserve the state of such historical works.

Forgotten Books is a registered trademark of FB &c Ltd.
Copyright © 2015 FB &c Ltd.
FB &c Ltd, Dalton House, 60 Windsor Avenue, London, SW19 2RR.
Company number 08720141. Registered in England and Wales.

For support please visit www.forgottenbooks.com

1 MONTH OF FREE READING

at
www.ForgottenBooks.com

By purchasing this book you are eligible for one month membership to ForgottenBooks.com, giving you unlimited access to our entire collection of over 700,000 titles via our web site and mobile apps.

To claim your free month visit:
www.forgottenbooks.com/free593945

* Offer is valid for 45 days from date of purchase. Terms and conditions apply.

English
Français
Deutsche
Italiano
Español
Português

www.forgottenbooks.com

Mythology Photography **Fiction** Fishing Christianity **Art** Cooking Essays Buddhism Freemasonry Medicine **Biology** Music **Ancient Egypt** Evolution Carpentry Physics Dance Geology **Mathematics** Fitness Shakespeare **Folklore** Yoga Marketing **Confidence** Immortality Biographies Poetry **Psychology** Witchcraft Electronics Chemistry History **Law** Accounting **Philosophy** Anthropology Alchemy Drama Quantum Mechanics Atheism Sexual Health **Ancient History Entrepreneurship** Languages Sport Paleontology Needlework Islam **Metaphysics** Investment Archaeology Parenting Statistics Criminology **Motivational**

THE EASTERN QUESTION.

A BRIEF HISTORY

OF

MONTENEGRO,

TO WHICH IS ADDED

A SHORT ACCOUNT OF BULGARIA, COMPILED FROM
MACKENZIE AND BAKER.

By GEORGE M. TOWLE.

BOSTON:
JAMES R. OSGOOD AND COMPANY,
Late Ticknor & Fields, and Fields, Osgood, & Co.
1877.

Co
By JAMES

FRANKLIN PRESS:
RAND, AVERY, AND COMPANY,
BOSTON.

CONTENTS.

MONTENEGRO:—

                                                                  PAGE

    INTRODUCTION 5

    I. HISTORY 7

    II. REIGNING PRINCE AND FAMILY . . . 25

    III. GOVERNMENT 27

    IV. PHYSICAL ASPECT, AREA, AND POPULATION, 31

    V. TOWNS AND VILLAGES 37

    VI. TRAITS AND CUSTOMS 41

    VII. MILITARY CHARACTERISTICS 50

BULGARIA:—

    I. RACE 61

    II. HISTORY AND CHURCH 66

    III. EDUCATION 80

    IV. TRAITS 93

MONTENEGRO.

INTRODUCTION.

THE fulness of the admiration which the civilized world lavishes upon a people resolute to maintain and defend their independence, belongs to that little, obscure, out-of-the-way niche of South-eastern Europe, which the Venetians set the example of calling "Montenegro," and its own inhabitants call "Tsernagora." Within the past two years we have seen this rugged and dauntless race once more asserting itself against overwhelming odds, holding a nation of fifteen millions at bay below its savage mountains, and, with its little army of twenty thousand, keeping in check the by no means despicable legions of the Osmanlis. Servia, its bigger neighbor, was quickly and easily subdued, and readily made peace, though Russian volunteers filled their ranks, and Russian officers led the onset. Montenegro held out stalwartly against the Turk: like many a Vladika before him, the young Prince Nikita stood with his petty army, at the entrance of his craggy passes, invincible.

This little Montenegro, indeed, is one of the most interesting countries in the world. Its history is full of the most romantic heroism; and obscure as that history is, preserved only by faint *piesmas,* or poetical traditions, it deserves a place beside the annals of Switzerland and of Sparta. Its aspect is ruggedly majestic; no scenery in Europe exhibits nature more vividly in its more sombre and awful manifestations. Its customs and habits are perhaps more curious than those of any people extant in Europe. Its religious and political institutions are not only well worthy the study of the ethnologist, but are replete with curiosities calculated to attract the cursory reader.

I.

HISTORY.

THE people of the Black Mountain await still their great epic bard, — their Virgil or their Homer. If such a one shall ever arise, — which is not perhaps probable for ages, since no people is more independent of literature, — he will find at his hand materials scarcely less ample for a glowing tale of glorious heroism, immense bravery, and wonderful self-sacrifice and submission to hardship, than did the Smyrnan and Mantuan poets in the majestic traditions of the Troad. For centuries Montenegro has never been wanting in whole families of Tells, in little legions of Achilleses, in heroes defending her many Thermopylæs with all the grim and Spartan gallantry of Leonidas. No people ever clung more obstinately to, or ever preserved more heroically against overwhelming odds, their independence. For three hundred years every Montenegrin has been a soldier, every priest a military leader, and every woman a *vivandière* or a nurse. The man of Montenegro ever sleeps on his arms. Every hill is a fortress, every mountain an immense barrier. To fight for his home and his arid and rocky soil, is as natural to this half-savage Christian as to eat and to sleep. Montenegro is a little, a very little, Switzerland; and the courage and patriotism of her sons are the more intense than those of the Swiss, as their domain is smaller, and their population huddled more closely together. Small as Montenegro is, a mere dot on the map, which only the eye practised in scanning maps can discover, a little ridge of crags between the narrow slip of Austrian Dalmatia and Turkish Albania, her history is brimming with romance; her traditions glow with the poetry of achievement, with deeds that thrill and strike with admiration and with awe. It is worth while to glance rapidly at that history, and to pass briefly in review the stirring events of the past three centuries, which are so many landmarks or monuments, telling the story of an unviolated national freedom.

In a work in this series recently published, I gave some account of the rise, power, and decline of the great Servian Empire, which rose in the fourteenth century, defied the Turks, made alliances with great European states, and was finally overthrown by the famous sultan Amurath, at the battle of Cassova, in 1389. Of this Servian Empire, which was at one time bounded by the Danube, the Adriatic, the Euxine, and the European Archipelago, Montenegro was a part, lying on its western limit. The population therefore was, and still is, Servian Sclavic in blood, and Greek in faith. After the carnage of Cassova, many of the Servians fled for refuge behind the impenetrable barriers of the Black Mountain. The rayah there found ample protection from his Moslem foe; and it may be added, that ever since that time, down to the present day, Montenegro has offered a home to exiles. Thither have fled Christians and Jews, and even Turks: under the protecting brow of the mountain you will find refugees of almost every creed, of Latin and Saxon as well as Tartar and Servian blood.

The governor of Montenegro under the last

Servian monarch, whose name was Balcha, and who had married the Servian king's daughter, declared the province independent, and set himself up as its ruler. For a long time, however, Montenegro contained no settled population. It was the sojourning place of Servian herdsmen and shepherds, of fierce brigands and marauders. These transient inhabitants lived without law, in the barbarian freedom of a primeval time. Then there arose a powerful and heroic prince, who lives in the memory and traditions of the Montenegrins as does Stephen Douschan among the Servians, Tell among the Swiss, the Cid among the Spanish, and Thor among the Scandinavians. Passing through the principality, you will find in the names given to springs and streams, to ruins, passes, caverns, and villages, the evidences of the fervid veneration of the people for Ivan the Black. Indeed, while some authorities assert that the name Montenegro, or " Black Mountain," was acquired from the dark aspect of the mountain ranges, others claim that it came from Ivan's cognomen, " Tsernöi " or " Black " There is a superstition among the Montenegrins, that

Ivan will one day re-appear as their liberator, a sort of political savior. They think he is not dead, but only reposing in a long slumber, from which he will at the proper moment arouse, and deliver them from their enemies. Ivan married an Albanian princess, and, having thus strengthened himself by a powerful alliance, proceeded with buoyant bravery to withstand the aggressive Turks. For already the victorious Mahomet II., Amurath, and his successor Bajazet, were resolved to add the Black Mountain to the territory dominated by the Crescent. Already had begun that long series of desperate assaults between the gigantic power of the Ottoman and the rude little bandit state, which was to endure to the present time, and which we see going on at this moment. Ivan succeeded in repelling Mahomet, the victor of Constantinople; thirty years later (in 1478) the sultan, bent on revenge, made a furious onset against his neighbor. This time he advanced into the Herzegovina, and, pushing Ivan back into his mountain fastnesses, threatened his complete overthrow. Ivan in vain appealed to the then powerful republic of Venice; and returned to the Black Mountain for a last desperate struggle. He burned the citadel of Jabliak, transferred the monks and treasures to Cettigne, and then constructed the frowning fortress which to this day defends the capital of the principality. Every Montenegrin was summoned to arms; and Ivan, calling the pride of his countrymen to his aid, declared that whoever should desert his post "should be despoiled of his arms, dressed in the garb of a girl, and handed over to the women, who should lead him about as a laughing-stock throughout the whole country, with spindles and a distaff by his side." Whether by reason of this edict, or of their natural rugged valor, it is certain that the Montenegrins under Ivan successfully resisted every attempt of the Turk to penetrate their fastnesses. So brilliant were Ivan's military exploits, that he was courted by Venice, married his daughter to the hospodar of Wallachia, and his eldest son to the daughter of the doge. It appears that the prospect of this latter marriage offended Ivan's subjects; and, fearing lest it might create trouble, he employed a stratagem. He had promised the doge that the family alliance should take place; and, when the time came for the bridegroom to go to Venice to seek his bride, Ivan sent another young man to personate him. The device was successful; and, when the bride reached Cettigne, the prince quietly took possession of her.

Throughout his reign Ivan had many times to resist the invasions of the Turks, always with brilliant success. His son and heir did not long enjoy the princely authority. His marriage had greatly offended his rude people, who looked upon the Venetians as heathen; he was not "a chip of the old block," and but languidly carried on the warfare with the Turks; and at last, finding his crown a thorny one and his princely position full of hardships and perils which his character was ill suited to bear, he yielded to the prayers of his Italian wife, abdicated, and retired to Venice, there to live out the remainder of his days in indolent luxury.

Well rid of this incompetent ruler, the Montenegrins hailed with delight the rise of a new and vigorous dynasty. Next to the prince, the man highest in dignity in Montenegro was the Vladika, or bishop. He happened to be a man of energy and warlike instincts, named German; adding to his religious office that of the political governorship, he founded the line of prince-bishops which descended to this century. "The offices thus combined," says an historian, "could not become hereditary, as the bishops of the Eastern Church never married; but the system was perpetuated, and it was arranged that the Vladika should be appointed either by popular election, or, as was afterwards the case, by the nomination of his predecessor." Under the Vladikas, the Montenegrins were almost constantly at war for two centuries; and they felt its humiliations and cruelties as well as its glories. More than once the Turks succeeded in penetrating the passes and occupying for a time the Montenegrin territory. Once the people were so far subdued as to be compelled to pay a poll-tax to the Grand Turk, "which was destined only to defray the cost of the sultan's slippers." During these Turkish occupations, many of the people embraced the faith of Islam; when the country again became free, the descendants of these apostates returned to the Greek communion, retaining, however, their Mussulman names, which still survive in Montenegro. The Turks, however, never remained long the masters of this stalwart race. The country always became in a short time too hot to hold them. They were surprised and massacred, driven into defiles and shot down troop by troop, and again and again expelled beyond the mountains. These alternate occupations and expulsions went on almost incessantly until the beginning of the eighteenth century. The country was a perpetual battle-field. Every town was a fortress. The country could not grow or produce: the men, herdsmen, priests, and all, were too busy fighting.

It was in the year 1703 — a year forever memorable to the Montenegrins — that this soil was at last rid of Turkish masters, and their scant pockets of the burden of Turkish taxes. Six years before, a bold, brave, and savage man, named Danilo Petrovitch, had been chosen Vladika by the people. He went to Hungary, where he was duly consecrated to the bishopric by the Servian patriarch; having already been aroused to a keen thirst for vengeance by the perfidy of the Turks, who had taken him prisoner by a stratagem, had grossly maltreated him, and had exacted a heavy ransom before restoring him to liberty. Danilo vowed that the Montenegrin soil should no longer be disgraced by the presence of the Moslem. He ordained a massacre as swift, as sudden, and as complete, as was that of St. Bartholomew. On the night of Christmas, 1703, under his instigation, the Montenegrins rose and slaughtered every Turk they could lay their hands upon in the territory. The next day they gathered in multitudes at their capital, Cettigne, where they gave themselves over to the wildest demonstrations of joy. The Turk, in his turn, dreamed of vengeance. Long and formidable were his preparations to again attempt the subjugation of the mountain province. Eleven years later the Turks advanced upon Montenegro, to be hurled back with frightful loss. Two years passed, and again they made the trial. This time they gained a partial victory, — won, however, not by a fair trial of arms, but by a base act of treason. They invited thirty-seven of the Montenegrin chiefs into their camp, promising them safety, for the purpose of negotiation. As soon as the chiefs made their appearance, they were seized and held as prisoners. Then the Turks, having deprived Montenegro of its ablest men, were able to penetrate the country and lay it waste, to burn the church and convent at Cettigne, and to butcher and carry off thousands of the inhabitants. But it was not safe to stay, and attempt to rule this dauntless people; the Turks retired, and for nearly half a century an armed truce continued between the two peoples.

It is doubtful whether the French and English courtiers of the time of Anne and the Fourteenth Louis had ever heard of such a place as Montenegro. Certainly Europe, up to that time, did not remember the existence of such a country. Peter the Great may be said to have discovered it; and that astute and enterprising sovereign was the first to recognize that the warlike dwellers in this mountain nook might be of use to him in his conflicts with the Turks. He sent to offer them his protection, and to engage them to join with him in fighting the Turks; and from that time to this — a period of more than a century and a half — the Montenegrins have lived under the ægis of Muscovite power. A singular event occurred in 1762, as a consequence of this alliance, or rather protectorate of Russia. In that year the czar Peter III. was strangled by order of the empress Catherine. Shortly after a man called "Stephen the Little," who had taken up his residence in a province adjoining Montenegro, and had practised there as a doctor, suddenly set up a claim that he was Peter III., having escaped the fate which was prepared for him. The Vladika of Montenegro scouted his pretensions; but Stephen, moving across the frontier into Montenegro, succeeded in completely persuading that superstitious people, and replaced the Vladika as the sovereign of the country. "So general was the credence given to the story," says Mr. Tozer, "that the Servian patriarch sent him a splendid horse as a present; and ultimately the Russian court found themselves obliged to take some steps in the matter, and sent a Prince Dolgorouki to denounce him as an impostor. On his arrival, the Vladika convened the chief men; and, when they heard from the Russian agent that Peter III. was certainly dead, at first they seemed disposed to believe him; but, when Stephen was afterwards confined in the upper story of the convent at Cettigne, he contrived to regain their confidence by a device which could only have succeeded with a very simple-minded people. He exclaimed to them, that they might themselves perceive that the prince acknowledged him to be the emperor, for otherwise he would not have placed him above himself, but beneath; and the effect of this declaration was so great, that Dologorouki was forced to leave the country without effecting his object. Stephen the Little ruled Montenegro for four years; but his reputation was impaired in a war with the Turks, in which he did not display the prowess that the mountaineers expected of him; and ultimately, having lost his sight in the springing of a mine, he retired into a convent, where he was murdered by his Greek servant at the instigation of the Pasha of Scodra."

Space does not permit that we should follow in detail the heroic struggles of the Montenegrins during the eighteenth and the present century,

— their valiant succor of the declining state of Venice when menaced by the Turk, victorious for the while in Bosnia and the Herzegovina; their noble triumph over Tchenghitch Bekir in 1727, and the later repulse of the Turks under Bey Loubovitch; the long blockade of Montenegro by Mehemet Begovitch; the ungrateful assault by the Venetians in alliance with the Turks, who once more broke into and ravaged the Montenegrin valleys; and the valiant part the mountaineers took in the Napoleonic conflicts, which sometimes raged close by them. We find always the same rude and dauntless courage, the same eternal resolve to be and to remain free; the same final victory in arms over the Moslem, obtained at fearful prices of carnage and desolation; the same dogged resistance to still greater powers, such as Austria and Russia, ambitious to absorb so brave a race into their own dominions.

The two last bishop Vladikas of Montenegro (for the political and the ecclesiastical powers were separated in 1851) were men of such conspicuous ability and virtue that we cannot avoid dwelling briefly upon their romantic careers. Peter the First, who succeeded to the Vladikate in 1777, would have worthily graced a far greater throne. He was a man of various and elegant accomplishments. He had been educated at St. Petersburg, had travelled a great deal, knew several languages, and was a keen observer of men. Assuming power, he soon proved himself an administrator of great vigor and resource: he re-organized his little state; he imparted something of discipline and training to his rude, brigand-like little army; and he energetically corrected the abuses incident to the lawless antecedents of the race. When war came, he showed that he was as brave and wise a soldier as he was an able governor. He defeated the Turks with great loss in 1796, when they invaded his territory, destroying almost their entire army, and killing the commander-in-chief. He acquired for Montenegro the district of the Berda; and by his victory at Kroussa he delivered his state for many years from the attacks of the Albanian Turks. At that battle he led his troops in person, and displayed such courage as to rouse his men to a perfect fury of valor. Peter was a most able diplomatist; and, when he saw that both Russia and Austria craved Montenegro, he played these powers off against each other, by arousing their mutual jealousy. He was a devoted son of the Greek Church; and when he died, at the age of eighty, after a reign of more than half a century, his people declared him a saint, and embalmed him in their hearts beside Ivan the Black. He was succeeded by his nephew, the pious and imaginative Peter the Second, a poet-priest, who earnestly pursued his uncle's projects of reform, and was scarcely less beloved as a ruler by the Montenegrins. Gentle in character, he yet showed himself capable of warlike prowess, and of an exalted patriotism. Two years after his accession, he defeated the Turks in the defile of Martinitch; and he indignantly refused the bribe of semi-independent luxury with which he was tempted by the grand vizier, replying that as long as his people would stand by him he would defend their independence. His reign was from first to last a troublous one. He had jealousies within his own dominions to subdue; he had to be ever on guard, as well against the perpetual intrigues as the always impending assaults of the Turks; he had to deal with the designs of the great powers. These he did with rare tact and uniform success. The last of the bishop-Vladikas is thus described · " He read much, spoke several languages, was distinguished as a Serb poet, and united in his person the qualities of a good soldier and an able diplomatist. He was probably the only bishop of his day who could hit with a rifle-ball a lemon thrown into the air by one of his attendants, — a feat which added not a little to the confidence he enjoyed among his troops. His appearance, too, was greatly in his favor; and his majestic height of about six feet eight inches might well command the respect of a primitive and warlike race."

Peter the Second was succeeded by Prince Danilo in 1851. Like his two predecessors, Danilo was an able man, earnestly bent on placing his state within the circle of civilized nations. It was he who separated the ecclesiastical from the political dignity of the Vladikate. While he remained a bishop, he could not, by the traditions of the country, marry. He had fallen in love at Trieste with a young Servian beauty: unwilling to give her up, he preferred to sacrifice his sacred office; which he did, and married her. His reign was vigorous but brief. He was assassinated at Cattaro in 1860, and succeeded by his nephew Nikita, the present Vladika, then eighteen years of age.

II.

REIGNING PRINCE AND FAMILY.

PRINCE NIKITA was born Sept. 13, 1841, and is one of the most interesting personages of our time. Educated at Paris, he is master of the German, French, Italian, and Russian languages. Nikita inherits all the fervor, bravery, and military tastes of his race. He is ambitious, and hopes, by the aid of Russia, to one day become the sovereign of a restored Servian kingdom. "Prince Nikita," says a recent tourist, "is handsome in person, frank and pleasing in manners, and possesses all the bearing of a true gentleman."

He was married in 1860 to Milena Petrovna Vucoticova, the daughter of one of the native Voivodes : she is one of the most beautiful women in Europe. She has never yet left the confines of her native land. Four children have been the issue of the marriage : three daughters, — Sophia, born in 1866, Militza, born in 1868, and Makie, born in 1869; and one son, Danilo Alexander, heir to the Validikate, born in 1871. The revenue of Prince Nikita is less than was that of his predecessors; and he now receives from his little state an income of only $1,850. He has, however, a considerable private income, and receives annual pensions, from the Emperor of Russia of $7,000, and from France of $10,000, with which he can live in some degree of comfort and state.

III.

GOVERNMENT.

The government of Montenegro is as simple as the habits of its people. It is virtually a republic, for each village elects its own chiefs, or mayors; and although the prince is nominated in each case by his predecessor, the affairs of the commonwealth are settled in a general assembly of the people. Individual liberty is jealously guarded: there is no restriction in the bearing of arms; and the right of free speech has been retained by the people from early times. The senate, which is composed of sixteen chiefs, is elected annually (the electorate consisting of such male residents as are at the time bearing or who have already borne arms), and to which all Montenegrins are eligible, is at once legislative and judicial. It is the only deliberative body, and is the highest law tribunal. Every peasant in the nation has the right of personal appeal to the prince for the redress of even the most trivial wrongs. A curious scene may be witnessed about half a mile from the town of Cettigne, on the afternoon of a summer's day. Here is a level lawn, enclosed by a semicircular formation of the rocks; at one end is a copse of low poplars. Under the largest of these poplars you may see two rows of wooden seats built, and a bench raised a little above them, against the tree. This is the famous "senate-house" of Montenegro. Here the senate meets in the open air, without the least ceremony. The prince presides over it, sitting on the raised bench; and the people come and stand around, behind the benches and on the rocks, to listen to the deliberations, to present their petitions, and even to mingle in the discussions of their conscript fathers. It is with some reason that the Montenegrins declare that they have "the largest senate-house in the world." Only within the past half-century has the Vladika had the power to punish even the gravest crimes. He could formerly only threaten the spiritual chastisement of his episcopal authority. In those times, therefore, every man took the law into his own hands; and the most desperate family feuds were kept aflame from generation to generation. Customs grew up, and had the force of law; and it is to the credit of the Montenegrins, that they learned in many cases to substitute, of their own accord, arbitration in place of the remorseless vendetta. The rise of several able and energetic Vladikas, who replaced the lawless freedom of the race by a series of established laws, and reduced the state to something like civilized order, gave a death-blow to many an old-time savage and bloody custom.

"The inhabitants," says a recent authority, "are divided into forty tribes, each governed by elective 'elders,' and a chief called Knjas, who acts as magistrate in peace, and as commander in war. For decision of important questions affecting the whole country, all the Knjas form an assembly, — the Skoupschina, — the decisions of which overrule both those of the prince and of the senate."

The Montenegrins are said to speak a purer Sclavic dialect than any other branch of the great Sclavic race except the Servians; and it may be noted that they possess an edition of the Bible which was translated into their tongue in the ninth century. They also claim to have more strictly preserved the traditions, tenets, and ceremonies of the ancient Greek Church than the Servians or the Roumanians. They pride themselves on their rigid orthodoxy; and it is highly to their credit, that, regarding as they do the Roman Catholic as "the dog's faith," they allow all Roman Catholics to remain perfectly secure within their territory. Indeed, though they hate the Turks so bitterly that they seize with delight every opportunity to fight them, there are many Turks resident in Montenegro; and these are disturbed neither in their persons nor in the free exercise of their religious rites.

IV.

PHYSICAL ASPECT, AREA, AND POPULATION.

It is difficult to find Montenegro on the map. Its name is seldom heard in the schoolroom; and it is only since the Eastern question became the vexed problem and skeleton-in-the-closet of Europe, that its name has often passed the lips of men. The Montenegrins have lived for centuries in a nook apart from the tide of civilization: while the rest of the world has been floating forward, Montenegro has remained stationary, moored out of sight. This small state, ruled over by a potentate who was formerly at once a prince and a bishop, lies near the edge, but not on the shores, of the Adriatic. In sight of that sparkling sea, the Montenegrin still has no port, and not a foot of strand where he has the right to settle himself. The Austrian province of Dalmatia, occupied by his Sclavic kinsmen, reaches down along the Adriatic coast, in a very narrow strip, and comes to a point and ceases a little south of Montenegro, extending just far enough to cut Montenegro entirely off from the sea. Dalmatia, therefore, is the western boundary of the principality. On the north it lies against the Herzegovina and Bosnia, Sclavic and Christian provinces of Turkey; on the east and south it is flanked by the larger and also Sclavic province of Albania. Turkey, therefore, hugs Montenegro on three sides, and Austria on the fourth; and for three centuries it has held its independence against both. The whole rugged territory ruled over by the Vladika, or prince, does not exceed two hundred and fifty square miles in extent; the number of his subjects is, as near as can be judged, one hundred and twenty thousand; and the fact that his army comprises one-sixth of the total population, that is, very nearly every able-bodied man in the country, shows what a thoroughly martial people his subjects are. The country is divided into eight *nahias*, or departments, in each of which are comprised several communes. They are ruled by governors, in conjunction with certain military leaders called "voivodas;" and both offices are confined to certain families, and descend from father to son.

In the whole principality you cannot count more than three hundred towns and villages. These are usually found in the valleys and on the slopes of the mountains. This, remarks an historian, "indicates the fearless independence of the Montenegrin, who feels secure in the natural strength of his country, and requires no measures of defence beyond his own courage." The largest town in Montenegro, moreover, does not contain more than fifteen hundred inhabitants.

The approach to the "Black Mountain" from the Adriatic is picturesque in the extreme. The neat little steamer which plies along the eastern coast of the historic sea first enters the bay of Cattaro, one of the most southerly towns and defences of Austrian Dalmatia. Cattaro lies along a strip close to the edge of the waters of the bay. Immediately behind it tower, in jagged and uncouth masses, a series of eminences which rise in the background till they attain the lofty peaks and summits of the Montenegrin mountains. Cattaro is a strange, quaint old fortress-town. Its turreted walls, its rampart and ditches, its castle frowning above on a rugged cliff, its narrow zigzag streets, its heavy gates, its curious bazaar, tell a story of antiquity and past vicissitude, as do many other towns on this western coast of ancient Greece and mediæval Servia. As the steamer winds into the irregular bay, you may discern from its deck, far up among the crags behind the town, a white serpentine path, which in the dim distance disappears between two peaks. That is the path to Montenegro. Ascending it, you find it far from an easy matter to reach the eyry of the hardy mountaineers. The path winds in zigzag fashion among the gloomy cliffs to a height of four thousand feet; and, the farther you ascend, the rougher and more difficult it becomes. To glance downward, and see the roofs of Cattaro at an immense distance almost perpendicularly below you, makes you grow dizzy and run in danger of losing your balance. Meanwhile, the higher you get, the more magnificent becomes the landscape on every side. The turnings of the bay come gradually into view; and, as you at last reach the topmost point of the path, the noble expanse of the glittering Adriatic is spread out before your delighted vision. Such a scene as that witnessed from this point is scarcely surpassed in Europe. Then you penetrate the awful defiles which lead to the interior of Montenegro. The glorious view of the bay and the sea vanishes suddenly from the sight; and you find yourself amid chaotic and stupendous piles of rugged rock, gray and gloomy, with but little vegetation and of most desolate aspect.

The traveller first reaches a plain among the mountains, which is dotted with a few very modest villages, and presents no special attractions. He hurries on to Cettigne, the capital, and finds that that supposably dignified place is approached from the plain by a simple pathway, which crosses a series of ridges grown with low shrubbery. Here and there are cattle browsing, with a boy acting as their herdsman; and occasionally men and women carrying wood to their cottages are met with. The country is composed of grayish-white rocks; and, although there are some wooded heights, the general aspect is that of a bald whiteness.

V.

TOWNS AND VILLAGES.

Cettigne is only seen when one is close upon it; for, to one coming from Cattaro, it is hid behind a jagged promontory. It lies in a plain, whence rise lofty peaks on every side. Two rather large and prominent buildings, the palace and the convent, are all that distinguish Cettigne from the mean aspect of the other Montenegrin villages; for the capital, after all, is but a village, and a far from large or handsome one at that. A single long street of two-story stone houses, at the end of which stands a large inn, and a wider street crossing it at midway, at right angles, leading to the palace: such is the modest Montenegrin capital. The Montenegrin villages, in truth, have all the humility of semi-civilization. They lie perfectly open upon the plain; the streets are but rude paths or lanes; the huts are scattered here and there without the least pretence of order or system; those which stand near each other have a rough common wall between them; and the houses themselves are of the most primitive and comfortless construction. They are built of stone, and have roofs that are either thatched or rudely shingled. Sometimes a house is seen with a tiled roof; and, as the Montenegrin usually dispenses with nails, the tiles are kept from being blown off by the tempests, by square blocks of stone placed on them at frequent intervals. The houses are most often a story and a half high. The half-story is a garret, or loft, where the master stores his corn and other provision for the winter. This is reached by a ladder which is placed in a rudely cut square hole; the floor of the loft is not seldom of wicker-work. Like the Roumanians and the Servians, the Montenegrin is satisfied with a single apartment for all domestic purposes. The single room on the ground floor is used as a dining-room, sitting-room, bed-room, and kitchen. He may be said to be perpetually "camping out" in his own house. He is "roughing it" all through his life. His bed is nothing but a rude bench, made of planks resting on a frame, and with a footboard. The poorer Montenegrin is content to throw himself upon this, and have his sleep out, with his clothes on; if he is rich, he provides himself with the luxury of a mattress; and some of them go to the extravagance of a quilt, and even curtains. The Montenegrin is one of the most social creatures in Europe; but his guest, if a native, must be satisfied to roll himself up in a rug, and sleep on the floor in the common apartment. It may be added that the Montenegrin very rarely disrobes, and always slumbers with his arms by his side. The whole population hold themselves forever under arms, in wait for the Turk. They make no toilet when rising; their first act is to light and smoke a pipe.

The fireplace is in the corner opposite what the Montenegrin is pleased to call his "bed." Before it is a raised hearth, and a caldron hangs from a ring above. Bread is baked, unleavened, in the ashes. There are no chimneys, and the smoke must get out into the air in any way it can. About the room are wooden benches, chairs, and tables. There are seldom any ornaments: a rude print is a luxury; clocks are unknown, and the Montenegrin ascertains the time of day by hour-glasses, or most often, indeed, by his skill in telling it by the position of the sun. "The only brilliant-looking objects in the house," says a traveller, "are the arms and dresses of the inmates."

VI.

TRAITS AND CUSTOMS.

THEIR mode of living is exceedingly frugal and simple. They eat the coarse bread baked in the ashes, this being made of Indian corn; they are fond of cheese and milk; and they consume a great many vegetables. Meat and fish are reserved for feasts and rare occasions; and the same may be said of wine. The Montenegrin is too poor to indulge in the luxuries of drink, and his poverty is the safeguard of his temperance. His chief extravagance is his dress; upon this he appears to lavish his savings with the prodigality of an American belle, or a shabby-genteel French dame who starves herself and freezes in order to appear in the fashions. He wears a white coat, or rather tunic, which reaches to the knees, is open in front, and is held about the waist with a sash. About the waist, too, is a leathern belt, from which hang his dirk and cutlass. Beneath his coat he has an ornamented red waistcoat and jacket. He wears loose, baggy trousers of a bright color, girt at the knee, and tight stockings, white worked gaiters, and heavy ox-hide shoes turned up at the ends; on his head is usually a small round cap, sometimes embroidered. Miss Mackenzie, in her "Travels," gives us a personal description of the Montenegrin men, which compels admiration of their physical qualities: "The lofty stature of these highlanders," says she, "their athletic proportions and warlike air, did not strike us more than the square brow and intelligent eye. They wear moustache, but not beard; the mouth and chin are firmly moulded; the teeth fine; the nose short but high; hair brown; large eyes, brown or blue, or oftener a dark gray — we seldom saw either hair or eyes black; the complexion is of a sunburnt red, rather than the dusky yellow of the Italian and Greek. They are larger men than the Tosk Albanians, even than the Gheggas; and they lack that unpleasing expression of cunning which strikes one in the Scodra (Dalmatian) people."

The Montenegrin women are mostly of medium height and build, square, solidly knit, and stalwart, with tough bronzed skins; having altogether the aspect of a race of women who are wont to share with the men their hardiest toils. They are often loaded with heavy burdens; but their step is firm, strong, and elastic. Their countenances, though so brown and tough, are not unpleasant. They are cheerful, modest, and intelligent. Now and then you see a Montenegrin beauty, "tall, with fine features and brilliant eyes;" but beauty is much rarer among them than the appearance of sturdy strength. In dress they are not more ostentatious, at least, than their husbands and brothers. Their dresses are short and often white; they wear short aprons and long veils, and love to deck themselves out with bright red embroideries. About their waists they wear heavy belts, which are often adorned with cornelians, set in a massive setting of silver, copper, or brass. Though the men are hardy and robust, they are apt to shift their burdens upon the women. "The sheaves of Indian corn, the bundles of wood, and every thing required for the house or the granary, are carried by the women: the men are supposed to be too much interested in the nobler pursuits of war or pillage to have time to attend to mean labors. I have seen," says Wilkinson, "women toiling up the steepest hills, under loads which men seldom carry in other countries." The men, it is true, till their not too fruitful valleys and slopes; but the burdens of the harvest are borne by the women, while their menkind loll about smoking their pipes. Indeed, the position of woman in Montenegro is scarcely more dignified or more free than that she holds in presumably more barbarous and Oriental Turkey. She is so sunk in submission to the lordly sex that she crouches before her master, kisses his hand and those of his stranger guests, with the conciliating humbleness of a dog. The Turk holds woman as a toy and caprice; the Montenegrin makes of her his slave and toiler. The latter, however, admits her as a companion and friend, which the Turk does not; and holds her in some respect and affection, as the mother of his children. Like the Oriental, he avoids all mention of his wife before a stranger; or, if forced to allude to her, apologizes for so doing.

As is the case with all the Sclavonic tribes, the Montenegrins make much of the marriage festival, despite the little honor in which they hold their women. They assemble from far and near to a wedding; they fire off guns and pistols, and make as much noise as possible with these and their stentorian voices; and then fall to eating and drinking, which lasts as long as the parents of the wedded pair can afford to supply the wherewithal. Petter tells us that "when a young man resolves on marrying, he expresses his wish to the oldest and nearest relation of his family; who repairs to the house of the girl, and asks her parents to consent to the match. This is seldom refused; but, if the girl objects to the suitor, he induces some of his friends to join him and carry her off; which done, he obtains the blessing of a priest, and the matter is then arranged with the parents. The bride only receives her clothes, and some cattle, for her dowry."

The Montenegrin, like the Swiss and other dwellers among mountains, is exceedingly hospitable. He welcomes a stranger guest with what the French would call "effusion:" his welcome, indeed, is somewhat too fervid. He seizes the new-comer, imprints hearty kisses upon his lips, and overwhelms him with hugs and caresses. As the guest approaches the house, a salute of guns is fired off in his honor; and, as the guns point downward in the direction he is coming, this method of greeting is not without its dangerous chances. If he points this out to his Montenegrin host, he receives the reply, that fate ordains who shall be killed and who saved; and that, if fate had intended him to be killed thus, it would have been all right. The stranger is regaled with all that the house affords, and implored to tarry as long as he chooses; and when he departs he is provided with a guide who will accompany him for miles on his way to his next destination.

The same poverty which forbids the Montenegrin an excessive indulgence in drink renders his habits and pastimes very simple. Almost the only musical instrument that he knows is the cithara, which is a sort of one-stringed lute, played with a bow, and producing a monotonous and rather lugubrious sound. Yet the Montenegrin minstrel, singing to its accompaniment in a loud, clear voice, the ballads which glorify the heroes of ancient Servia, makes a music weird indeed, but not discordant or unpleasant to hear. Their games are but few: their chief delight is war; and they often indulge in the recreation of descending upon some Turkish village beyond their mountains, and pillaging it, at the same time cutting off the heads of its chief men, and bearing them home as trophies of their valor. Their amusements are of the most robust. Quoit-pitching and bowling are in vogue, and they are proud of their nimbleness in jumping and other gymnastics. They also pride themselves on a somewhat curious accomplishment, that of being able to shout very loudly. Their voices are exceedingly strong, and their pronunciation very distinct. One writer says that two Montenegrins can keep up an intelligible conversation at a distance of half a league from each other; and another, the author of "A Ramble through Montenegro," relates an anecdote worth repeating: "We passed a village at a small distance, and lay on our oars to hear the news. Most of the people were absent; but one, a great man, was seated on a hut-top, with a few idlers round him. This was the chief president of the senate, the speaker of the house, in short; and undoubtedly, if stentorian lungs are of any use for that office in a Montenegrin parliament, he was most amply qualified. For twenty minutes this eminent man conversed with us, the distance at first being about a quarter of a mile, and probably it might be three miles or more before he was finally out of hearing."

The Montenegrins are very superstitious. They never pass a church without repeatedly crossing themselves; and, after doing murder without stint among their Turkish neighbors, will piously raise a cross where a murder has been committed, and solemnly make the sign of the cross every time they go by it. They believe in the agency of evil spirits in bringing misfortunes upon men; and they have a dismal way of howling with their iron lungs at funerals. It is singular to visit a country where horses are a rarity, and where such a thing as a wagon is seldom seen. Not many years have elapsed, indeed, since horses were introduced into Montenegro by the Vladika Danilo; and then it became necessary to import Italian masters of horsemanship to teach the chief men how to ride. Of cattle, however, there are plenty. One of the chief industries is that of herdsman; and, while the Montenegrins faithfully cultivate every patch of tolerable soil they can find amid their jagged cliffs, they find the raising of sheep, cows, goats, and pigs, more profitable. Such a thing as manufacturing industry is unknown among them. Fishing is the most lucrative occupation next to farming and grazing, unless, indeed, we include as an occupation the brigandage against the Turks, from which few refrain.

VII.

MILITARY CHARACTERISTICS.

There are about twenty-two thousand Montenegrins, between the ages of twenty and fifty, capable of bearing arms. There is no standing army; but every subject who is capable is trained to arms, and expected to bear them if called upon.

"The arms of the Montenegrins," says Miss Mackenzie, "consist of guns, pistols, and yatagans, or long knives, for cut and thrust, worn in their girdles; and the Vladika has lately introduced some rifles and a few cannon. Their guns are very long, and carry to a great distance; the slender stocks are often inlaid with mother-of-pearl or steel ornaments, and the locks are flint and steel. They have no matchlocks. They are very good marksmen; and their unerring shot is quickly followed by the use of the yatagan, when they can close with their enemy. Their mode of fighting is generally from behind rocks, when their foes are numerous; and the nature of their country enables them to adopt this mode of warfare to great advantage."

The following account of the Montenegrin warlike customs and methods is that of M. Borniewski, an eye-witness of some of their operations against the Turks:

A Montenegrin is always armed, and carries about, during his most peaceful occupations, a rifle, pistols, a yatagan, and a cartouch-box. The Montenegrins spend their leisure time in firing at a target, and are accustomed to this exercise from their boyish years. Being inured to hardships and privations, they perform without fatigue and in high spirits, very long and forced marches; they climb the steepest rocks with great facility, and bear with the greatest patience hunger, thirst, and every kind of privation. When the enemy is defeated and retiring, they pursue him with such rapidity that they supply the want of cavalry, which it is impossible to employ in their mountainous country.

Inhabiting mountains which present at every

step passes where a handful of brave men may arrest the progress of an army, they are not afraid of a surprise, particularly as they have on their frontier a constant guard ; and the whole of their force may be collected, within twenty-four hours, upon the threatened point. When the enemy is in great force, they burn their villages, devastate their fields, and, after having enticed him into the mountains, they surround him, and attack him in a most desperate manner. When the country is in danger, the Montenegrins forget all personal feelings of private advantage and enmity ; they obey the orders of their chief ; and, like gallant republicans, they consider it a happiness and a grace of God to die in battle. It is in such a case that they appear as real warriors ; but, beyond the limits of their country, they are savage barbarians, who destroy every thing with fire and sword.

Their ideas about war are entirely different from those adopted by civilized nations. They cut off the heads of those enemies whom they take with arms in their hands, and spare only those who surrender before the battle. The property they take from the enemy is considered by them as their own, and as a reward of courage. They literally defend themselves to the last extremity. A Montenegrin never craves for mercy; and whenever one of them is severely wounded, and it is impossible to save him from the enemy, his own comrades cut off his head. When, at the attack of Clobuk, a little detachment of our troops was obliged to retreat, an officer of stout make, and no longer young, fell on the ground from exhaustion. A Montenegrin, perceiving it, ran immediately to him, and, having drawn his yatagan, said, "You are very brave, and must wish that I should cut off your head: say a prayer, and make the sign of the cross!" The officer, horrified at the proposition, made an effort to rise, and rejoined his comrades with the assistance of the friendly Montenegrin. They consider all those taken by the enemy as killed. They carry out of the battle their wounded comrades on their shoulders; and, be it said to their honor, they acted in the same manner by our officers and soldiers.

Like the Circassians, they are constantly making forays in small parties, for the plunder of cattle, and consider such expeditions as feats of chivalry. Being safe in their habitations, where nobody dares to molest them, they continue their depredations with impunity, disregarding the threats of the Divan, and the hatred of their neighbors. Arms, a small loaf of bread, a cheese, some garlic, a little brandy, an old garment, and two pairs of sandals made of rawhide, form all the equipage of the Montenegrins. On their march they do not seek any shelter from rain or cold. In rainy weather the Montenegrin wraps his head with the *strooka*, lies down on the ground, and sleeps very comfortably. Three or four hours of repose are quite sufficient for his rest, and the remainder of his time is occupied in constant exertion.

It is impossible to retain them in the reserve ; and it seems they cannot calmly bear the view of the enemy. When they have expended all their cartouches, they humbly request every officer they meet with to give them some ; and, as soon as they have received them, they run headlong into the farther line. When there is no enemy in sight they sing and dance, and go on pillaging ;

in which we must give them the credit of being perfect masters, although they are not acquainted with the high-sounding names of contribution, requisition, forced loans, &c. They call pillage simply "pillage," and have no hesitation in confessing it.

Their usual manner of fighting is as follows: If they are in great force, they conceal themselves in ravines, and send out only a small number of shooters, who, by retreating, lead the enemy into the ambush; here, after having surrounded him, they attack him, usually preferring on such occasions swords to fire-arms; because they rely on their personal strength and bravery, in which they generally have the advantage over their enemies. When their numbers are inferior, they choose some advantageous position on high rocks; where, pronouncing every kind of abuse against their enemies, they challenge them to combat. Their attacks are mostly made during the night, because their principal system is surprise.

However small their force may be, they always try to wear out the enemy by constantly harassing him. The best French *voltigeurs* on the advanced posts were always destroyed by them; and the enemy's generals found it more advantageous to remain under the cover of their cannon, of which the Montenegrins were not at all fond. However, they soon became accustomed to them, and supported by our rifles they bravely mounted the batteries.

The tactics of the Montenegrins are confined to being skilful marksmen. A stone, a hole, a tree, offer them a cover from the enemy. Firing usually in a prostrate position on the ground, they are not easily hit, whilst their rapid and sure shots carry destruction into the closed ranks of a regular army. They have besides a very praetised eye for judging of distance; they thoroughly understand how to take advantage of the ground; and as they usually fight retreating, the French, who took it for a sign of fear, constantly fell into their ambushes. As for themselves, they are so cautious that the most skilful manœuvres cannot deceive them

Their extraordinary boldness frequently triumphed over the skill of the experienced bands of the French. Attacking the columns of the enemy in front and flank, and acting separately without any other system than the inspirations of personal courage, they were not afraid of the terrible battalion fire of the French infantry.

The Montenegrins cannot withstand regular troops beyond their mountains, because, destroying every thing with fire and sword, they cannot long keep the field ; and the advantage of their courage in assisting our troops, and the fruits of victory, were lost by their want of order. During the siege of Ragusa, it was never possible to know how many of them were actually under arms, because they were constantly going to their homes with spoil, whilst others joined the army in their places, and, after a few days of indefatigable exertion, returned to the mountains to carry away some insignificant trifle.

It is impossible to undertake any distant expedition, and consequently to accomplish any thing of importance, with them. In one respect, they have a great advantage over regular troops, — by their great skill in mountain warfare, although they are completely ignorant of the military art.

In the first place, they are very lightly dressed, are exceedingly good marksmen, and reload with much more rapidity than regular soldiers. The Montenegrins dispersed, and deliberately firing from a lying position on the closed rank of the enemy, are not afraid to attack columns composed of one thousand men, with numbers not exceeding one hundred or one hundred and fifty.

In a pitched battle, their movements can be ascertained only by the direction of their standards. They have certain signal cries, which are uttered when they are to join in a compact body for attacking the weaker points of the enemy. As soon as such a signal is given, they rush furiously onward, break into the squares, and, at all events, create a great deal of disorder in the enemy's ranks. It was a terrible spectacle to see the Montenegrins rushing forward with heads of slaughtered enemies suspended from their necks and shoulders, and uttering savage yells. They can be employed by a regular army with great advantage, for fighting on the advanced posts, for seizing the enemy's convoys, destroying his magazines, &c.

The Russian commander-in-chief had much difficulty in persuading them not to cut off the heads of their prisoners. He finally succeeded not only in this (chiefly by paying them a ducat for every prisoner), but, what was more difficult, in persuading them, with the assistance of the Vladika, to embark for an expedition on board ship; a thing which they had never done before. Notwithstanding that they were treated with the greatest kindness, they proved very troublesome guests. Whenever the captain invited their chiefs to breakfast, they all entered the cabin; and, having observed that more dishes were served to officers than to common sailors, they wanted to have a similar fare. When the fortress of Curzola was taken, and the feast of Easter was approaching, they gave the captain no repose, entreating him to accelerate his return to Cattaro; but when it was explained to them that the vessel could not advance against the wind, they fell into great despondency.

When at last the ship approached the entrance of the Bocca di Cattaro, and they caught a sight of their own black mountains, they uttered joyous acclamations, and began to sing and dance. On taking leave, they affectionately embraced the captain and the officers, and invited those to whom they had taken a liking to pay them a visit. But when the sailors told them they could not leave the ship without the permission of their superiors, they were much astonished, and said, "If you like to do a thing, what right has another to forbid you?"

Such are Montenegro, and its past and present rulers and condition. The fate of the sturdy, half-savage little state is probably at stake in the approaching settlement of the Eastern question. It is Servia's rival in the ambition to become the centre of a re-united Servian and Sclavic nationality, and to see its prince the restored successor of Stephen Douschan.

BULGARIA.

I.

RACE.

From Misses Mackenzie and Irby's interesting work on the "Sclavonic Provinces of Turkey in Europe," I take the following graphic sketch of the history, institutions, and characteristics of the Bulgarians:—

"By Bulgaria we understand, not that insignificant portion of the same termed the Turkish province of Bulgaria, but the whole tract of country peopled by Bulgarians. The population, usually given as four millions, is estimated by the people themselves as from five to six millions,— forming the eastern division of the South Sclavonic race.

"The Bulgarians are distinguished in all essentials from their neighbors, the Greek, the Rouman, and the Turk. They differ in a few points of character from their own western kindred, the Groasto-Servians. The chief of these latter points is a deficiency in what is called '*esprit-politique*,' and a corresponding superiority in the notion of material comfort. Unlike the Servians, the Bulgarian does not keep his self-respect alive with memories of national glory, nor even with aspirations of glory to come: on the other hand, no amount of oppression can render him indifferent to his field, his horse, his flower-garden, nor to the scrupulous neatness of his dwelling.

"How strongly difference of race can tell under identical conditions of climate, religion, and government, is exemplified in towns where Greeks have been dwelling side by side with Bulgarians for centuries.

"The one is commercial, ingenious, and eloquent, but fraudulent, dirty, and immoral: the other is agricultural, stubborn, and slow-tongued, but honest, cleanly, and chaste. The latter qual-

SHE STOOPS TO CONQUER,

AND

THE GOOD-NATURED MAN.

ity has from early times attracted respect toward the South Sclavonic peoples. Their ancient laws visit social immorality with death; and at present their opinion, inexorable towards women, does not, like our own, show clemency to men.

"A lady told us, that in the society of Greeks she could not be three weeks without becoming the confidante of a *chronique scandaleuse:* among Bulgarians she had lived for months, and never heard a single story.

"In Bulgarian towns the Mussulmans are Osmanli colonists, who form, as it were, the garrison of the province The Sclavonians who have become Mahometan mostly live in the country, and continue to speak Sclavonic.

"In their bravery and warlike disposition, the renegade Bulgarians evince the character of the nation before it was betrayed and disarmed, and they themselves adopted Mahometanism only to avoid falling into the position of rayahs. In some parts they are known by the name Pomak (from Pomagam, 'I help'), and are supposed to be descended from those Bulgarian troops who served in the Sultan's army as 'allies' until the

Turks grew strong enough to force on them the alternative of surrendering their arms or their creed. Among our guards once happened to be a Bulgarian Mussulman, who allowed us to be told in his presence that he was still at heart a Christian; and in the neighborhood of Salonica we heard of Mahometan Bulgarians who excuse their apostacy by the following story : —

"Being hard pressed, they fixed a certain term during which they would fast and call on Christ, but at the end whereof, if no help appeared, they would submit themselves to Mahomet. Help arrived not, so Mahometans they became. Since then, old hatred of race has caused them to take part against the Greeks in more than one insurrection; but they equally detest the Turk, and thus sympathize with their own Christian countrymen in their national antipathies, as well as in tenacity of their native tongue.

"The rural population of Bulgaria is Christian; and hereabouts the rayah has a down-look and a dogged stolidity, which give one the impression that heart and mind have been bullied out of him. Of late years, however, he has presented an unflagging resistance to the Porte's imposition of foreign bishops; and those who have instructed him, both in his own country and out of it, assured us that he is of excellent understanding, and zealous and apt to learn. The Christian Bulgarian is reproached as timid, but at least his is the timidity of shrinking, not of servility. He hides from those he fears: he does not fawn on them.

"His country, lying as it does on the road of Turkish armies to the Danube, has been subject to unceasing spoliations; and nothing is more melancholy than the tale told by its desolate highways, and by the carefulness with which villages are withdrawn from the notice of the passers-by. Cross the border into Free-Servia, and the cottage of the peasant re-appears.

II.

HISTORY AND CHURCH.

"To give a sketch of Bulgarian history, one must go back to the end of the fifth and beginning of the sixth century, when a Sclavonic population south of the Danube is spoken of by Byzantine authors.

"Under the old East Roman Empire, the people of Bulgaria appear both as subjects and as rulers. Justinian's birthplace was, as it still is, a Sclavonic village in the neighborhood of Skopia; and his Latin name is the translation of his Sclavonic one, Upravda. The great Belisarius is said to have been the Sclavonic Velisar; the emperor Basil and his line were Sclaves. It would appear that the first colonists established themselves to the south of the Danube gradually, and recognized the imperial rule; but in the seventh century they were joined by tribes of a more warlike character, under whose leadership they rose against Byzance, and overran the greater part of the peninsula.

"Who these new-comers were, is still matter of discussion. Most commentators declare them Tartars, who, on adoption of Christianity, amalgamated with the Sclaves; but some Bulgarians will have it that they were brother Sclaves emigrating from beyond the Volga, and consider it impossible that a race of foreign conquerors should have been absorbed so completely and so soon.

"Whoever they were, from them dates the name of Bulgaria, and the first dynasty of her sovereigns. Though often at war with the Byzantine Empire, the Bulgarians profited by its neighborhood so far as to imbibe a certain amount of civilization. In the ninth century, they fought covered with steel armor; their discipline astonished the veterans of the empire; and they possessed all the military engines then known.

"Their kings and czars encouraged literature, and were sometimes themselves authors. As almost all accounts of them come from Byzantine sources, there can be little doubt that this portrait is not flattered. Under their more powerful rulers, the Bulgarians threatened Constantinople; under the weaker, they acknowledged the Byzantine emperor as suzerain; and more than once Byzantine armies effected a temporary subjection of their land; but their monarchy was not finally overthrown till the end of the fourteenth century, when they were conquered by the Turks.

"Coins of Bulgaria are to be seen in the museum of Belgrade; and a curious chronicle of czar Asen has lately been published in modern Bulgarian.

"At the Turkish conquest, 1390, Shishman, the last king of Bulgaria, surrendered himself and his capital to the conqueror's mercy; but the people submitted only by degrees, and always on the condition that, if they paid tribute to the sultan, they should be free to govern themselves.

"Their soldiers were commanded by their own voivodes; their taxes were collected, and towns and villages ruled, by officers of their own choosing.

"The Bulgarian Church had native bishops, and

a patriarch residing first at Tirnova, then at Ochrida. All this is proved by firmans and berats accorded to them by numerous sultans.

"Those who take the scraps of liberty nowadays octroyed to the rayah, as evidences of a radical change in the maxims of Turkish rule, should bear in mind that far better terms were accorded by Turks to Christians five centuries ago.

"Those who put faith in Turkish promises should inquire how the liberties guaranteed to such Christians, as submitted to the first sultans, came to be trampled under foot so soon as the Turks could call themselves masters of the land.

"Of the Bulgarian voivodes the most resolute were cut off, and the rest left to choose between emigration and apostacy. In 1776 the autonomy of the Church was destroyed; and, in place of native bishops of one interest with the people, Greeks were sent from Constantinople, who plundered the peasants, denounced the chief men to Turkish suspicion, set an example of social corruption, and burnt all Sclavonic books and manuscripts whereon they could lay their hands.

"The last schools and printing-presses found shelter in the Danubian principalities; when those lands came under Phanariot government, nothing was left to the Bulgarians save some old convents in the recesses of their hills.

"Few points are more remarkable, in the history of Ottoman rule, than the mode in which Turks and Greeks have played into each other's hands. The sultan could never have crushed the heart out of his Christian subjects without the aid of a Christian middle-man; and the Greek has used the brute force of his Mohammedan employer to complement his own cleverness and guile.

"Under the later emperors Greek dominion was unknown in Sclavonic and Rouman lands; whereas, under Ottoman sultans, we find Greek prelates and Phanariot princes ruling the Rouman, the Bulgarian, and the Servian. That nationality must be of tough material which gave not way under this double pressure.

"The first break in the prison-wall was made by the revolution at the beginning of this century. 'Free Greece, autonomous Servia: may not Bulgaria have her turn?' Gradually the wealthier Bulgarians sent their sons for education no longer to Constantinople, but to Russia, Bohemia, France.

"In the country itself were founded native schools; and even in districts already half Hellenized the national spirit began to revive. Persons who used to write their own language in the Greek character learned late in life the Sclavonic alphabet; and we have ourselves seen parents who spoke Bulgarian imperfectly, anxiously providing that their children should know it well.

"It was the obstacle presented by a foreign hierarchy to these efforts at national development, that brought the people to the resolution of freeing their Church from the control of the Phanar.

"This temper was taken advantage of by the Roman propagandists; and emissaries were sent all over Bulgaria, promising self-government and services in Sclavonic, with no other condition than that a nominal recognition of the patriarch should be exchanged for that of the pope. This condition cannot be called hard; and at its first start the Romanist propaganda was a success. The number of converts has been hugely exaggerated;

yet it doubtless included some persons of influence.

"But the principal bait to the adoption of Catholicism was the promise of sharing the protection of France; and when it became evident that this protection could not be unlimited, nor exempt its *protégés* from payment of taxes, the new-made Romanists recanted in troops.

"Then, too, their leaders became convinced that the movement could have no other effect than to extend to Bulgaria what had already broken the strength of Bosnia and Albania, i.e., a Latin sect, — separated from the other Christians, cowering under foreign protection, selling its assistance to the Turks.

"With these views (we give their own version of the story), and not from any religious sentiment of scruple, many to whom the propaganda owed its first encouragement withdrew their aid, and opposed it with all their might.

"But the indifference wherewith the common people had talked of transferring ecclesiastical allegiance proved to the thinkers in Bulgaria that the dangers of division might at any moment recur. For the second time in their church history, it was recognized that the South Sclavonians would remain in the Eastern Church only on condition of ecclesiastical self-government. If they are to have foreign bishops or a foreign head, it is all one to them whether their pope resides at Constantinople or Rome.

"At this juncture, deputies from Bulgaria made their appearance in Constantinople. They came to demand that, in virtue of the *hatti humayoun*, their national patriarchate, formerly recognized by the Porte, should be restored; or at least that their church be declared autonomous, with native archbishop, bishops, and synod, and an ecclesiastical seminary at Tirnova.

"In short, they desired such a system of church government as succeeds admirably in the principality of Servia. It is years since the Bulgarians put in their claim; but the Turk is in no hurry to remove a cause of quarrel between his Christian subjects.

"With great subtlety he has tried to improve the occasion by hinting to the Bulgarians that they had better secede from the Eastern Church.

They have been told that by the treaty of Adrianople the Greek patriarch is declared head of all the orthodox communities in Turkey.

"'Be Catholic,' says the Mohammedan judge, 'or Protestants, or set up a sect of your own, and we will recognize you with pleasure: so long as you call yourselves "orthodox," we must know you only as Greeks.'

"But the Bulgarians avoided the snare. They replied that their demand affected no religious question; that they had no desire to separate themselves from the orthodox communion. They were perfectly ready to yield the Greek patriarch recognition as head of the Eastern Church: to be its *only* patriarch, he had never aspired.

"His predecessors had acknowledged a patriarch of Bulgaria till within the last ninety years; he himself at the present moment recognized patriarchs of Jerusalem and Antioch. Besides, the practical settlement of the business depended, not on the patriarch, but on the padishah.

"When the Bulgaria patriarchate was abolished, it was by authority of the sultan: to this day no prelate throughout the Ottoman Empire can exercise his functions without an imperial firman; and such a firman is all that a Bulgarian primate, already chosen by the people, is waiting for in order to appoint his bishops, convoke his synods, and regulate internal affairs. Give him this, and the Greek patriarch may defer his recognition so long as it suits his own convenience, while without a firman the recognition of the Greek patriarch would be of no practical effect.

"This statement places the Ottoman Government in an attitude somewhat different from that which has been claimed for it; for it has been usually represented as striving vainly to reconcile Christians in a religious dispute wherein it may mediate but not interfere.

"No doubt, however, the Greek Patriarch might have done much to avoid an appeal to Mohammedan authority, and would have best consulted the interests of his own community by agreeing to accept the proffered recognition together with a fixed tribute.

"But it must ever be remembered that, in a post so important as that of the Constantinopolitan chair, none but a pliant agent is tolerated by the

Turk. Certain it is, that the patriarch then in office behaved equally unworthily and unwisely. Three bishops (Hilarian, Accentios, and Paissios) had declared themselves ready to resign their sees in Bulgaria, unless confirmed therein by the choice of the people. They might have been used as mediators : on the contrary, they were seized and sent into exile.

"All such Bulgarians as did not accept the patriarch's terms were anathematized and declared heretics.

"By such measures the formidable wrath of a slow, stubborn people has been thoroughly roused. The patriarch who excommunicated them, they have renounced ; rather than receive his bishops, communities declare they will remain without any ; should a Greek venture to impose himself upon them, they resist him by every means in their power.

"A series of scandals took place throughout the provinces. Churches were closed in order that the Greek liturgy might not be read therein. When the Greek bishops returned from their revenue-gathering progresses, they found their palaces locked, and were conducted beyond the city walls.

"If they entered a church to officiate, no Bulgarian priest would take part in the service; when they departed, the floor was ostentatiously swept, as if to remove traces of impurity. In Sophia, when a new bishop was expected, men, women, and children filled the palace, and blocked it up, till, unarmed as they were, they had to be expelled by Turkish soldiers.

"The bishop then dwelt in isolation, until, on occasion of a burial, he got hold of a Bulgarian priest, and demanded why he did not come to see him. The priest answered that he must stand by his flock; that, as it would not acknowledge the bishop, neither would he. Thereupon the priest's beard was shorn, the fez of the dead man stuck on his head, and he was turned out of the streets as a warning and a sign.

"Again the unarmed citizens rose: shops were shut, houses evacuated; thousands of people prepared to leave Sophia. Their elders waited on the pasha and said, "Either the Greek bishop must go, or we."

"The pasha advised the prelate to withdraw; and, as the authorities in Constantinople would not permit the people to elect a new one, Sophia resolved to do without a bishop at all.

"At Nish, a town on the Servian frontier, the bishops anticipated an inimical demonstration by accusing the elders of the Bulgarian community of a plot to join the Servians. The elders were called before the pasha, and without a hearing, without being allowed to say farewell to their families, or to send home for extra clothing, they were hurried into carriages, and sent off into banishment.

"This occurred in the depth of winter; and when, in the ensuing August, we were hospitably received by the family of one of the exiles, they besought us to apply to some English consul to learn if their relatives were yet alive.

"Meanwhile a variety of evils pressed on Bulgaria, — outbreaks of haidooks, some political outlaws, some highwaymen; influx of Mohammedan Tartars from the Crimea, for whom the Bulgarians were forced to build houses and provide food; emigration of Bulgarians to Russia, succeeded by their destitute return; attempt of other Bulgarians to get off to Servia, frustrated by the Turkish authorities; finally a shoal of Bashi-Bazouks turned loose among the villagers, on pretext of guarding the frontier from the Servians.

"In the summer of 1862 we were witnesses to this state of things. Another means resorted to for holding down the Bulgarians is the introduction of Mahometan colonists, who replenish the declining Mussulman population, and are kept well supplied with arms, of which the Christian is deprived.

"Since the Tartars, Circassians have been introduced; and the idea has been adopted of planting them along the frontier of Servia, so as to bar off the Bulgarians. The Tartars were only idle, whereas these new immigrants come thirsting to avenge their own sufferings on all who bear the Christian name.

"It is said, however, that the Circassian mountaineers do not thrive on the Bulgarian plains, and are rapidly decreasing in number.

III.

EDUCATION.

"THE mountain chains of the Balkan and the Rhodope divide Bulgaria into three sections, — northern, central, and southern. Of the northern district, between the Balkan and the Danube, we cannot speak from eye-witness, as the Turks declared it too disturbed for travellers; but we say, on the authority of persons who have lived there, that those Bulgarians who grow up with the great water-way of commerce on one side of them, and their natural mountain fortresses on the other, are more independent and enterprising than their brethren on the inland plains.

"Here, too, the people maintain numerous schools, of which the best are at Tirnova and Shumla. Tirnova, the ancient capital, is the site proposed for an ecclesiastical seminary, and if possible, for a printing-press, both of which the jealousy of the Porte as yet denies.

"Central Bulgaria is that which lies between the ranges of the Balkan and the Rhodope. Here we visited the schools of Adrianople, Philippopolis, Samakoff, Sophia, Nish, — all supported and managed by the Christian communities without pecuniary aid from the government of bishops.

"The schoolhouses, mostly of good size and airy, are, like every thing in Bulgaria, clean. The schoolbooks, gathered from various sources, are eked out with those of the American Board of Missions.

"To conciliate the Turks, Turkish is frequently taught to a scholar or two; and phrases complimentary to the sultan have been framed into a sort of school-hymn. True, the same tune has another set of words in honor of him who shall deliver the country from Turkish rule.

"One or other version is sung before the visitor, according as he is judged to be Christian or Turkophile. We had opportunities of hearing both.

"At Philippópolis, Samakoff, and Sophia, there are girls' schools. That at Sophia is the best, and was founded by a patriotic citizen. In his own words, "When my wife died, and left me but one son, I resolved not to marry again, but to give all my money and attention to this school." He has brought a female teacher all the way from the Austrian border, for Sclavonic schoolmistresses are hard to find in Turkey. The missionaries at Eski Sagra have a Bohemian, who keeps their girls' school as full as it will hold.

"Southern Bulgaria lies, as we have already indicated, between the Rhodope and the frontiers of ancient Greece. Such schools as we there visited were smaller and poorer than elsewhere; but we did not see those of Istib and other towns lying on the more northerly route between Salonica and Skopia. Those on the line of our journey we will notice as we proceed.

"Throughout the places we have hitherto mentioned, the Greek bishop contents himself with ignoring the Bulgarian school, or from time to time expelling an energetic teacher; but nearer the Græco-Sclavic boundary, we found Sclavonic education positively impeded. In Vodena and Yenidjé, a Greek school is founded, and the community must needs support it. In case poverty should not be sufficient to deter them from supporting also one of their own, every possible hindrance is thrown in the way.

"One result of this anti-national policy is, that the Bulgarians, elsewhere so eager to learn, are in these districts listless and dull; another result is, that being alienated from their own clergy, they lend an ear to overtures from Rome. Some of them calculate on using Latin aid to get rid of the pope; others still fear that the yoke they know not may prove heavier than the yoke they know.

"In Monastir the Unionists have a school, and at Yenidjé they are building a church. The name Unionist is given to communities which retain the Oriental rite while they acknowledge the supremacy of Rome."

The efforts of patriotic Bulgarians to keep alive their language, and, by perpetuating it, to maintain the national spirit of the race, have been to a large degree successful. Col. James Baker describes this remarkable educational movement, and gives us its results during the past twenty-seven years, as follows: —

"Subscriptions were raised in all the district towns; and teachers were imported from Russia and Austria. The movement was denounced by the Greek patriarch, and every device and intrigue were used to crush it. But the funds which had been raised cleared away the opposition of the Ottoman authorities, and permission was obtained to establish schools distinct from those of the Greeks in some of the district towns; and the first central school was triumphantly opened in Philippopolis in 1850.

"Be it observed, that this success was due to the exertions of the upper class of Bulgarians, — a class which had been extinguished at the conquest of the country, but which was slowly but steadily revived by the industry of the people.

"From the opening of the central school at Philippopolis dates the revival of popular education amongst the Bulgarians.

"It struggled with difficulties until the Crimean war; but after that event it spread with amazing rapidity, and exhibited an amount of potential energy for national development which is truly wonderful.

"The Sandjak of Philippopolis was the central and controlling province of the Bulgarians in Thrace. It contains a population of 664,000, composed of

Bulgarian Christians	390,000
Mohammedans, principally Bulgarians	240,000
Greeks, Albanians, and Wallachs	10,000
Jews, Armenians, and Gypsies .	24,000
	664,000

"It has 14 towns, 877 villages, and 109 *tchiflliks*, or private farms.

"Two-thirds of the villages are occupied by Bulgarians; and most of the farms are worked by them.

"It is a part of this district which has been the scene of the unhappy massacres during the late disturbances, which were brought about, not by the Bulgarian people, but by Russian intrigue.

"Prior to 1850, reading and writing were considered rare accomplishments in this province; and there were hardly any schools for teaching the Bulgarian language. Before the close of 1858 there were 5 central, 8 preparatory, and 90 elementary schools, besides 7 girls' schools: total, 110.

"In eight years, viz., in 1865, there were 6 central, 25 preparatory, 180 elementary, and 18 girls' schools: total, 229.

"In 1870 there were 1 gymnasium or central college, 6 central, 25 preparatory, 281 elementary, and 24 girls' schools: total, 337.

"There were 16,500 pupils; viz., 13,885 boys, and 2,615 girls, with 346 male and 39 female teachers.

"The progress was still more rapid until the date of the Servian war, and the anarchy produced by the so-called Bulgarian rebellion of 1876.

"When we consider the apathy of the Ottoman Government, and the active persecution of the Greek patriarchate, the rapidity of this educational advance cannot but excite our admiration.

"The course of instruction in these schools had

a modest commencement, but increased in scope with the advance in education.

"At first, difficulty was found in obtaining teachers; but the difficulty was promptly met by the establishment at Philippopolis of a special training-school for teachers.

"In the central schools the course of instruction extends over five years, and includes the Bulgarian, Turkish, Greek, and French languages, practical arithmetic, elementary mathematics, geography, Bulgarian and Turkish history, religious and moral instruction, and church music. I visited the school at Eski Sagra, which contains over five hundred boys and three hundred girls, and they were admirably managed; the buildings were spacious, clean, and well ventilated, and the students cheerful and well dressed and very intelligent.

"I was also a guest for a few days of the schoolmaster at Troyan, a town north of the Balkan (which doubtless derives its name from Trajan), and was much struck with his intelligence and the admirable management of his school; and I have seen many others to which the same description would apply.

"In the gymnasium established at Philippopolis 1867–68, by special imperial sanction, besides the subjects taught at the central school, mental and moral philosophy are added; and students are sent to it from the lower schools to complete their studies.

"In the preparatory school, the course of instruction extends over four years. They are divided into two divisions, the upper and lower.

"In the girls' schools, reading, writing, and needle-work are taught; and children of the poorer class enter at five or six, and study until twelve years of age, while those of the upper class remain up to fourteen, but seldom over sixteen years of age.

"In the central schools, boys remain up to seventeen, and sometimes to nineteen years of age.

"At first the teachers were selected from Bulgarians educated in Russia; but they were immediately denounced to the Ottoman authorities by the Greeks, as spies from that country: so it was found expedient to obtain the supply of teachers from Bulgarians educated in Turkey.

"The teachers are liberally paid, their salaries ranging from $350 to $700 per annum. They possess much influence with the country people, and are a great source of national union.

"Education is free for rich and poor, who sit side by side in friendly rivalry.

"Up to the year 1860, the school funds were derived from voluntary subscriptions and from funds bequeathed by charitable persons; but it was found that the administration of such funds was unsatisfactory, and that they were frequently misappropriated.

"A very important change then took place, and one which foreshadowed the rapid approach of the revival of an independent Bulgarian church.

"The Bulgarians of Philippopolis, as usual, led the van, and renounced their allegiance to the supremacy of the Greek patriarch at Constantinople; and they followed up this bold step by appropriating the ecclesiastical domains, tenements, and revenues of the diocese, and immediately employed a part of their funds for educational purposes. Other districts in the province soon followed the lead; and each contributed a certain number of chosen men to form a central board for the management of the ecclesiastical and educational interests of the province.

"An excellent organization was the immediate result; and it was determined that a mixed commission of clerical and lay members should be elected annually in each district, charged with the immediate direction and control of its affairs, both local and ecclesiastical, and that each commission should act as a separate board, independent of the other, but responsible to the community at large for the supervision and promotion of public instruction.

'As a matter of course, all these important changes were not made without the passive sanction of the Porte, and the amount of patience and perseverance which brought them about cannot easily be measured; but, at the same time, we must credit the Ottoman Government with the progress which they at all events permitted to be carried out by their subjects.

"We thus see that the Bulgarian school fund is supported by voluntary contributions and bequests; but there is a peculiar exception, and one which is quite novel to the practice of the country. The gymnasium at Philippopolis derives its funds from a direct tax annually levied on each Bulgarian "Nefouz," male inhabitant of the kasa, or district, at the rate of fifty-two paras (5c.) per head. This school rate is compulsory, and is assessed by the Ottoman authorities under a special firman, and by them applied to the maintenance of the college.

"The tax produces about thirty-five hundred dollars per annum, and is willingly paid by the inhabitants. We here get a government tax, the proceeds of which are given as a government grant to a non-Mahometan national school, an innovation which was only carried in 1868 after much agitation on the part of the Bulgarians.

"The Ottoman authorities frequently attend, by invitation, the public examinations and delivery of prizes at the Bulgarian schools.

"The craving for education amongst the people is very great; and I was surprised to find that at a little village near the Black Sea coast at which I was staying, one of the Bulgarian rayahs, who had raised himself to comparative independence by his own agricultural industry, built at his own expense a very good schoolhouse, and provided a schoolmaster, for the benefit of the village community."

IV.

TRAITS.

I TRANSLATE from M. Boué's excellent work on "La Turquie d' Europe," the following description of the salient traits of the Bulgarians, as contrasted with those of the Servians, Bosnians, and Montenegrins.

The very prominent and square forehead of the Servian and the Bosnian betrays benevolence and goodness, united with courage, firmness, and often foresight, as well as generosity. They are more apt to calculate the chances of disaster before rushing upon danger, than the Greek.

If they are fond of economizing and saving, they have less personal ambition ; and, if they are as proud of their country and race as is the Greek, they do not bore strangers, generally avoid lying and exaggeration, and are modest enough not to boast of their great deeds. They only ask for peace, tranquillity, and that no outsider whatever should interfere with their affairs.

The Montenegrins rather deviate from this trait, and like, they say, to paint their exploits in glowing colors.

The Bulgarians, especially those who live on the plains, do not possess the valuable qualities of the Servians to any large degree. They are good-natured, humane, and economical; they are less averse to work than their neighbors, and more submissive to all government than the Servians and the Bosnians; but, like the Russians, they seem to like pleasure and recreation better. They are wanting in courage and a deep sentiment of nationality, which only survives among their brothers of the western Balkans, and the mountains of High Mæsia and of Macedonia.

In those regions the Bulgarian is almost the equal of the Servian, and he only needs sturdy and patriotic chiefs. The heroic songs of the Servians are the fashion among them as well as in Servia; whilst on the Danube tender or festive refrains are oftenest to be heard.

PLEASE DO NOT REMOVE
CARDS OR SLIPS FROM THIS POCKET

UNIVERSITY OF TORONTO LIBRARY

H&SS
A
6144

WITH MAPS.

UNIFORM WITH THE "EASTERN QUESTION."

Cloth, 50 cents; Paper, 25 cents.

IN a compact form this "Brief History of Russia" presents those facts about the Russian people and empire, which everybody just now desires to know. The history of the successive dynasties is succinctly related in connection with the extension in territory, and the advance in civilization made by the empire. The important social and political changes that have occurred within the present century, and especially the circumstances of the Crimean war, and the chain of events that have led Russia to declare war against Turkey, are presented with clearness and precision. Excellent Maps add to the value of this timely book.

THE EASTERN QUESTION

HISTORICALLY CONSIDERED.

With Notes on the Resources of Russia and Turkey,
and an Abstract of their Treaties with
the United States.

By JAMES M. BUGBEE.

Vol. 18mo.   With Maps.   Cloth, 50 cts. ; paper, 25 cts.

In this timely book Mr. Bugbee gives just the information everybody desires for a satisfactory understanding [of] the causes of the war between Russia and Turkey. [It is a] compendious and very clear narrative of the previous relations between these two countries, and of the treaties and combinations employed to keep the peace between them; so that the reader has in a nutshell the facts necessary to a comprehension of the points at issue, and how they have been brought into issue.

The present government of each country is described, with its resources and its capacity for war.

The treaties made between these countries and the United States are summarized.

This little book, full of compact and luminous information, and supplied with good maps, is emphatically a book for the hour.

JAMES R. OSGOOD & CO., Publishers,

Lightning Source UK Ltd.
Milton Keynes UK
UKOW01f1341120717
305174UK00007B/171/P